OCEANIC SOCIETY EXPEDITIONS
& EARTHTRUST

FIELD GUIDE

to the

HUMPBACK WHALE

Hannah J. Bernard

&

Michele Morris

Parviz

May the whales
enchant us
always.

Aloha
Michele Morris

SASQUATCH BOOKS
Seattle

Printed in the United States of America.
01 00 99 98   5 4 3 2

Cover design and illustration: Dugald Stermer
Interior illustrations: Sandra Noel
Maps: Karen Schober
Composition: grafX

Library of Congress Cataloging in Publication Data

Bernard, Hannah J.
   Field guide to the humpback whale/Hannah J. Bernard & Michele Morris
      p. cm. — (Sasquatch field guide series)
   Includes bibliographical references
   ISBN 0-912365-93-5
   1. Humpback whale — North Pacific Ocean. 2. Whale watching—North Pacific Ocean. I. Morris, Michele, 1951–   . II. Title. III. Series
   QL737.C424B47   1993
   599.5'1—dc20   93-26808

Published by Sasquatch Books
615 Second Avenue, Suite 260
Seattle, Washington 98104
(206) 467-4300
books@SasquatchBooks.com
www.SasquatchBooks.com

Other titles in the Sasquatch Field Guide series:
The Oceanic Society
Field Guide to the Gray Whale
American Cetacean Society
Field Guide to the Orca
Adopt-a-Stream Foundation
Field Guide to the Pacific Salmon
The Audubon Society
Field Guide to the Bald Eagle
Great Bear Foundation
Field Guide to the Grizzly Bear
International Society of Cryptozoology
Field Guide to the Sasquatch
The Greater Yellowstone Coalition
Field Guide to the North American Bison
Western Society of Malacologists
Field Guide to the Slug
People for Puget Sound
Field Guide to the Geoduck

Contents

Introduction   5

A Word About Whales   7

Humpback Whale Facts   9

Diet and Feeding   14

Vocalizations   16

Humpback Behavior   18

Annual Life Cycle of the Humpback Whale   21

Hunting the Humpback Whale   25

Saving Humpbacks   26

Whalewatching from Shore   28

Whalewatching by Boat   29

Photographing Humpbacks   31

Whalewatching Guide   33

Sites
    Alaska   35
    British Columbia   37
    Washington, Oregon, and California   37
    Mexico   41
    Hawaii   43

Whale-Sighting Log   45

Suggested Readings   46

Information Sources   47

ACKNOWLEDGMENTS

The authors wish to thank the following people for their assistance: Kenneth Balcomb, John Calambokidis, Suzanne Canja, John Ensign, Deborah Glockner-Ferrari, David Hack, Ron LeValley, Dan McSweeney, Sally Mizroch, Mike Nolan, Sally Nolan, Lesley Segedy, and Birgit Winning.

Partial proceeds from the sale of *Field Guide to the Humpback Whale* go to the following organizations:

OCEANIC SOCIETY EXPEDITIONS

Oceanic Society Expeditions is a nonprofit organization that promotes education and research related to a variety of significant environmental issues. Begun in 1972, OSE is the educational and field research travel affiliate of Friends of the Earth, a worldwide environmental advocacy organization. For many years, Friends of the Earth has taken an international approach to such global environmental problems as ozone depletion and ocean pollution. Oceanic Society Expeditions addresses these concerns by offering people a chance to learn about conservation issues firsthand, through participation in study programs and research expeditions.

EARTHTRUST

Earthtrust is a nonprofit international organization dedicated to wildlife conservation and environmental preservation through a combination of field activities, education, research, and corporate partnerships to protect the environment. Save the Whales International, a program based in Maui, Hawaii, trains naturalists for whalewatching excursions, provides educational programs about marine life to local schools and resorts, and sends a conservation representative to meetings of the International Whaling Commission.

Introduction

Many animals of the temperate and subtropical regions of our world undertake annual migrations between their summer and winter habitats. Perhaps none of these migrations are better witnessed than those of the great whales—sea mammals that traverse thousands of miles to find suitable environments for feeding and breeding.

Among these giants is the humpback whale, or *Megaptera novaeangliae* ("great-winged New Englander," so named by New England researchers for the whale's immense pectoral fins). Humpbacks are distributed worldwide, migrating long distances from polar feeding grounds to tropical breeding grounds and back. In the North Pacific, humpbacks travel some 6,000 miles (9,600 km) between their winter and summer homes. The largest concentration of the North Pacific humpbacks can be found in the Hawaiian Islands during the winter months. Although it was speculated for many years that humpbacks that bred in Hawaii fed in cold, nutrient-rich waters somewhere near the Aleutian Islands, it wasn't until the late 1970s that their summer feeding grounds were actually pinpointed.

We now know that the North Pacific humpback population is distributed among three geographically separate breeding and feeding areas. The subpopulation or stock found wintering south of Japan in the Ryukyu Islands, the Marianas, the Bonins, and Taiwan is known as the Asian or western North Pacific stock. They probably feed in the eastern Bering Sea, west along the Aleutians. The central North Pacific stock winters in Hawaii and feeds off the coast of southeastern and south-central Alaska, in the Gulf of Alaska. The eastern North Pacific stock winters off western Mexico, Baja, and the Gulf of California, with a small number found as far south as Central America. They feed along the coasts of northern California,

Oregon, and Washington. Only a few individuals have been known to travel between central California and Hawaii within a given year; fewer still are known to travel between Mexico and Hawaii in a given season.

Humpback whales are the most active and exciting of the baleen whales to observe. During breeding season, the males engage in aggressive competition over females, bashing each other with their powerful tail flukes, hurling their 40-ton bodies against each other, and creating unique and mysterious songs. Females are also quite active, pec-slapping and breaching, engaging in violent displays against unwanted suitors, and nursing and instructing their young. These behaviors can be seen from land and sea, particularly in Hawaii, Mexico, and Alaska.

This book will serve as a guide for those who wish to view these phenomenal animals, whether whalewatching on vacation or as a vocation, viewing from land or from aboard a boat. Our goal in this book is to provide basic knowledge about the biology, migration, conservation, and history of the humpback whale of the central and eastern North Pacific, in order to assist the veteran whalewatcher and novice alike. We hope to spark your curiosity and enthusiasm, too, as we share with you our awe of these magnificent leviathans.

A Word About Whales

During the past 20 years, public interest in and scientific understanding of marine mammals have virtually exploded. At the same time, the world's populations of whales and dolphins have struggled to recover from centuries of exploitation by humans. The dwindling numbers and vast range of these creatures make obtaining information about them challenging. Just when we become fairly certain about a generalization or two, we discover a new piece of the puzzle that dashes our assumptions. We still have much to learn.

Paleontologists have helped cetologists group whales, dolphins, and porpoises into one order, Cetacea, with two suborders, Mysticeti and Odontoceti. The mysticetes, or baleen whales, are ocean grazers with baleen plates (made of a keratinaceous protein much like our fingernails) extending from their upper jaws, which strain food from the sea. Humpback whales are mysticetes, as are the gray whale and the blue whale. The odontocetes are toothed whales and are predators, sometimes hunting and tracking their prey in packs, like wolves, with the aid of biological sonar or echolocation. Killer whales (orcas), beluga whales, dolphins, and porpoises are examples of toothed whales. However, new information continues to challenge this classification scheme. For example, although paleontologists and anatomists classified the sperm whale as an odontocete, current genetic research places the sperm whale in closer relation to the baleen whales than to the toothed.

The humpback belongs to the family of mysticetes known as balaenopterids. The early Norse whalers dubbed this family the "rorquals," or red whales, for their characteristic throat grooves: when a whale is feeding, these grooves expand and appear pinkish in color. Between 5 million and 12 million years ago, the modern rorquals were already plying the North Pacific. The largest of all whales, the blue, is another rorqual, as

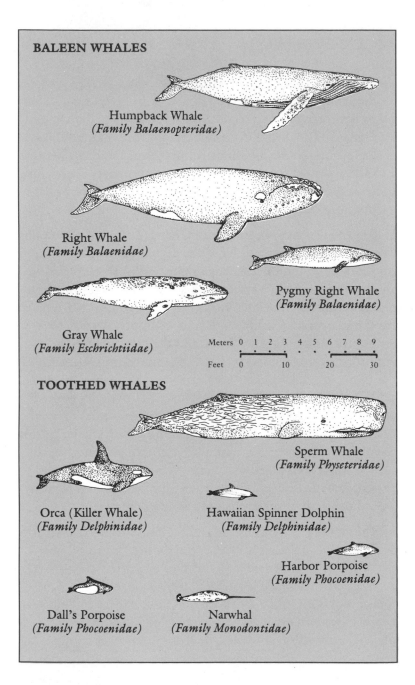

BALEEN WHALES

Humpback Whale
(Family Balaenopteridae)

Right Whale
(Family Balaenidae)

Pygmy Right Whale
(Family Balaenidae)

Gray Whale
(Family Eschrichtiidae)

Meters 0 1 2 3 4 5 6 7 8 9

Feet 0   10   20   30

TOOTHED WHALES

Sperm Whale
(Family Physeteridae)

Orca (Killer Whale)
(Family Delphinidae)

Hawaiian Spinner Dolphin
(Family Delphinidae)

Harbor Porpoise
(Family Phocoenidae)

Dall's Porpoise
(Family Phocoenidae)

Narwhal
(Family Monodontidae)

are the fin, the sei, Bryde's, and the smallest baleen whale, the minke. Other characteristics rorquals share are long, slender bodies, a distinct ridge on the top of the head, and a dorsal fin placed well back on the body.

Humpbacks are easily distinguished from their relatives. As their scientific name suggests, they have the longest pectoral fins (informally known as flippers); they also have a distinctive dorsal fin and flukes (flukes are the fins that form the tail), and knobs called tubercles, or stove bolts, on their heads and chins.

Humpback Whale Facts

SIZE	A medium-size baleen whale, slightly stockier than other balaenopterids. Females are slightly larger than males, attaining an average length of 45 feet (13.7 m); males average closer to 42 feet (12.9 m). Adults weigh between 25 and 40 tons (22.8–36.4 t). Average length at birth is 14 feet (4.3 m), weight about 2 tons (1.8 t).
LIFE SPAN	At least 48 years confirmed, probably longer.
DISTRIBUTION	Widely distributed in all oceans, ranging from the tropics, where they breed mostly in the waters around islands or continental coasts, to the edges of the polar pack ice. There appear to be three geographically isolated populations, referred to as the North Pacific, the North Atlantic, and the Southern Ocean groups.

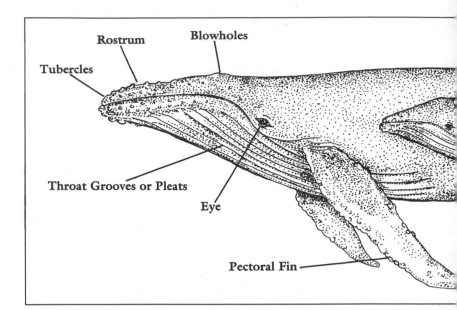

Tubercles

Rostrum

Blowholes

Throat Grooves or Pleats

Eye

Pectoral Fin

COLOR

Upper body is slaty gray to black. Lower is highly variable; can be white or black on the undersides of the flukes and pectoral fins, and on the region between tip of chin and ventral grooves. Southern hemisphere humpbacks can be nearly all white. Rostrum and region under the mouth can be mottled white with barnacles and scars from barnacles, as well as scars from fights.

BLOWHOLES AND BLOW

Paired, as with all baleen whales. The blow is a strong, bushy V-shape when viewed head-on, columnar when seen from the side, usually at least 6 feet high (1.8 m). Feeding humpbacks habitually blow four to eight

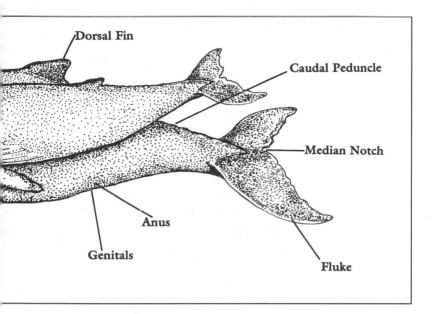

Dorsal Fin

Caudal Peduncle

Median Notch

Anus

Genitals

Fluke

times at intervals of 15 to 30 seconds before beginning a long dive.

DORSAL FIN

The base of the dorsal fin is wide, almost steplike, situated a little more than two-thirds of the way back on the whale's body. At the beginning of a deep dive, the whale hunches its back in the dorsal fin area, hence the designation "humpback."

PECTORAL FINS

Humpbacks have the longest pectoral fins, or flippers, of all of the whales, measuring an average of 15 feet (4.6 m), nearly a third of body length. Like the trailing edges of the flukes, the flippers' leading edges are knobby and scalloped. The bones in the flipper are

11

very similar to human arm and hand bones, but with greatly elongated phalanges (fingers). Humpbacks are quite dexterous with their pectoral fins, using them to herd fish, caress their young, maneuver, and loudly slap the water's surface.

FLUKES

The shape of the flukes is an identifying characteristic of the humpback. The rear margin has a slight S-curve and many knobby scallops. Average fluke width is 15 feet (4.6 m). Distinctive to the humpback species is a pattern on the underside of each whale's tail that is as unique to the individual as our own fingerprints are to us. The pattern ranges from all dark to all white, with a whole gamut of splotching, scarring, and scalloped edges in between. Researchers use these patterns to recognize individuals.

SWIMMING AND DIVING

Typical cruising speed is 1.5 to 4 knots, but humpbacks can attain burst speeds of approximately 20 knots. A normal dive stays within 200 feet (60 m) of the surface; estimated maximum dive is 485 feet (148 m). Normal duration of a dive is 4 to 9 minutes, but occasionally longer than 15 minutes. As they dive, humpbacks frequently throw their flukes high into the air, exposing the white or partially white undersurface and the rippled rear margin.

VOCALIZATIONS	The most sophisticated vocalizer of all baleen whales. (See separate section "Vocalizations.")
PREDATORS	Orcas, tiger sharks, and humans.
PREY	Like all baleen whales, humpbacks are filter feeders, with a more varied diet than some. They consume many species of krill (euphausiids), as well as several types of fish. (See separate section "Diet and Feeding.")
PARASITES	Two major types of external parasites reside on humpback whales. Barnacles attach themselves to the flippers, throat, chin, head, and flukes. As the whale grows, so do the barnacles, becoming embedded in new layers of skin. Many barnacles die and fall off the whale in warmer waters. Although barnacles are filter feeders and do not feed on the whale's tissue, cyamid crustaceans, or whale lice, cling to barnacle-encrusted areas and in skin folds, where they feed on the whale's sloughing skin. Like all whales, humpbacks have a number of internal parasites as well.

Diet and Feeding

Of all of the baleen whales, humpbacks display the most diverse and spectacular feeding styles. Their diet is varied, though feeding seems to be restricted to the periods whales spend in colder waters. Humpbacks in the southern hemisphere feed largely on abundant Antarctic krill; the northern hemisphere menu can additionally include planktonic crustaceans and a wide variety of schooling fish, such as sardine, mackerel, anchovy, and capelin.

The central and eastern Pacific stocks seem to separate into geographically isolated feeding aggregations on their summer grounds, with some whales returning to the same general area and feeding together over the course of many years. In southeastern Alaska, where the feeding behavior of humpbacks has been studied for nearly 20 years, at least two different strategies have been noted: long-term associations among individuals feeding cooperatively on schools of fish, and variable aggregations of individuals feeding on plankton swarms.

Bubble-Net Feeding

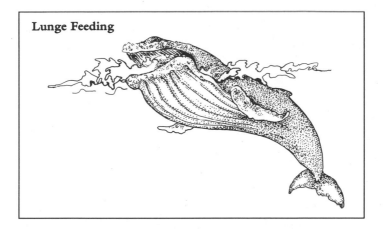

Lunge Feeding

Humpbacks may have devised their cooperative method of catching fish because fish are fast, evasive prey. When feeding on fish shoals, a cooperative group of up to 40 whales will lunge and dive synchronously through the fish, often with one whale feeding close beside another in a side-lunge out of the water, echelon-style. A single whale may initiate feeding by swimming in a spiral below the fish school, streaming bubbles from its mouth (humpbacks gulp air for this endeavor) or blowhole. These bubbles rise like a curtain or net to corral the prey. The whales then lunge through the confused mass of fish, further herding them with their long pectoral fins. They may also stun fish with mighty slaps of their flippers or flukes.

In areas where the ocean is alive with swarming krill, single animals can feed easily and efficiently without cooperative grouping. A whale might engage in flick feeding—swimming near the surface and flicking its tail up and forward to force prey toward its mouth. Or the whale might simply lunge and gulp its way through the highly concentrated, slow-moving prey. Like all rorquals, the humpbacks have extensive throat grooves that expand during feeding. One whale can take in more than 500 gallons (1,900 liters) of prey and water in a single lunge, then tighten the throat muscles to expel the water through the baleen, and retain up to 100 pounds (45 kg) of food in the mouth. An average humpback may consume 3,000 to 4,000 pounds (1,364–1,818 kg) of food per day!

Vocalizations

Although whales produce at least some sounds, humpbacks have the widest known repertory of all baleen whales. The majority of humpback sounds are very low tones (below 1,000 hertz), with higher sounds reaching about 4,000 hertz. (Toothed whales make use of even higher frequencies.) The varieties of humpback sounds have been characterized as low moans, groans, roars, snores, and surface ratchets; modulated wavers, *oos, ees, whos, wos,* and *foos;* abruptly changing *yups, mups,* and *ups;* and high chirps and cries. The famous humpback "song" is made up of short phrases arranged in specific patterns to create themes. A variety of themes are strung together in a sequence averaging about 15 minutes in duration. The sequence is usually repeated, sometimes for hours. It is not known for certain how humpbacks produce their sounds. Whales do not have vocal cords, and no air is released while humpbacks sing.

Why do humpbacks sing? Theories abound: songs may be warning signals for other whales, means of marking territory, a courtship technique, or aggressive display. Singing (so far noted only as a male activity) generally occurs in warm-water breeding areas, rarely in colder feeding areas. Singing has also been recorded over substantial distances of the migration routes. Audiogram tracings of songs indicate that each herd essentially has its own song, and all singers in each semi-isolated stock sing their own approximation of it. All singers in the herd incorporate new themes and eliminate old ones almost simultaneously, even over vast areas (e.g., Hawaii to

Mexico), so the song is transformed to some degree by the end of the breeding season. Whalewatchers use a hydrophone (a microphone designed to be submerged in water) to listen to the whales. Snorkelers and scuba divers can hear whale songs *unaided* if the singer is within 5 miles (8 km). It is estimated that other whales can detect the general range of a humpback's song from at least 19 miles (31 km) away, and the very lowest-frequency tones from a distance of at least 115 miles (185 km).

Whales are inclined to rise for breathing at the same point in the song, giving the experienced whalewatcher the opportunity to identify the singer if the whale is visible. For the most part, singers have been observed as lone whales positioned about 11 yards (10 m) underwater with the head lower than the flukes. However, male escorts accompanying a cow and calf have also been observed singing.

During feeding, humpbacks may use some extremely loud vocalizations to manipulate schools of fish, facilitating their capture. The sounds may also announce the presence of prey to other whales in the vicinity. The 50- to 90-second feeding call includes three or four quick ascending phrases at the end that increase in volume. This vocalization has been referred to as the "trumpet call"; its use has been observed in non-feeding situations as well.

Social vocalization has been noted during aggressive male-male interaction in courtship groups. Such sounds probably are demonstrations of dominance or agitation as adult males compete for access to a female. It's further speculated that animals may vocalize when they come together and again when they split into separate groups. Some research seems to indicate that mothers and calves also communicate using vocalization.

Humpback Behavior

SPYHOPPING

When spyhopping, the humpback slowly rises, bringing its massive head as much as 10 to 12 feet (3–4 m) vertically out of the water, to the point where its eyes are above the surface. It is believed that the whale's vision is well adapted to both air and water—sometimes the animal will turn on its axis, appearing to look around. At the end of this graceful maneuver, the whale slips back into the water, leaving behind only the tiniest of ripples.

BREACHING

In breaching, a humpback propels itself with a couple of powerful strokes of the flukes from 10 to 20 feet (3–7 m) below and parallel to the surface upward in a vertical or oblique motion, rising out of the water and crashing back down with a thunderous splash. The pectoral fins sometimes balance, twist, or position the animal in the air as it prepares to land on its back or side. The whale might execute a belly-flop, exhaling at the peak of the jump. Perhaps the most acrobatic of the baleen whales, humpbacks are also among the most frequent breachers. The whales appear to breach in a variety of circumstances and for a number of possible reasons, including social interaction, exercise, body language, and as an announcement of their presence that is both visible and audible (as in response breaching, when separate whales breach repeatedly asynchronously, sometimes miles apart). Breaching also supplies a means of looking around the surface, pounding off barnacles, and aiding digestion.

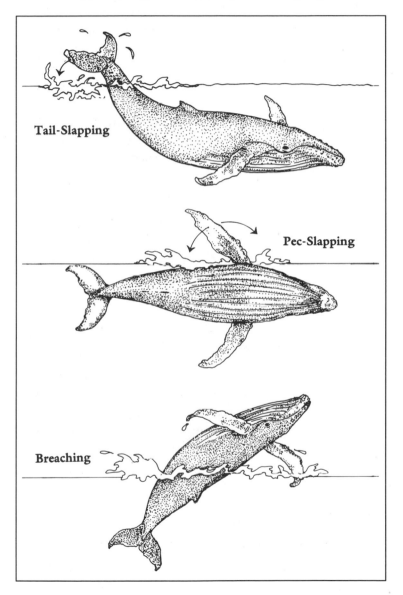

Tail-Slapping

Pec-Slapping

Breaching

PEC-SLAPPING Pec-slapping appears to be a form of body language or signaling that is invitational rather than aggressive. The whale lifts one long pectoral fin out of the water as it lies on its side (sometimes exposing one fluke), then slaps it down on the surface, creating a loud cracking sound. Whales have also been observed on their backs with both flippers extended upward, waving them about before rolling and smacking them on the surface.

TAIL-SLAPPING In this forceful display, the whale extends its flukes above the water as it lies either belly-up or belly-down under water, balancing with the pectoral fins extended to either side for balance. The tail then slaps the surface, often repeatedly, creating a tremendous sound and an explosive splash. Very likely this is a form of communication or possibly a means of warning.

SOUNDING After a series of blows and short surface dives, a humpback will eventually descend for a longer, deeper dive called the sounding dive. As it prepares for the descent, the whale rises, dramatically arching its spine in the area of the dorsal fin, rounding the region of the tail stock, and rolling the body downward. Usually, the whale then lifts its flukes above the water for a final thrust.

Annual Life Cycle of the Humpback Whale

ALASKA AND NORTHERN CALIFORNIA FEEDING: APRIL–OCTOBER

During the summer months, humpbacks of the central North Pacific stock spend most of their time feeding and resting in the frigid, subarctic waters around Alaska or along the North American coast as far south as California. The long days of summer enhance the growth of phytoplankton in these waters, and the increase of this microscopic algae, which is at the base of the oceanic food chain, leads in turn to an abundance of zooplankton. Zooplankton is what the whales come to eat. In fact, the humpbacks' migration is perfectly timed to coincide with the growth of this abundant food source.

Although the exact route between the whales' breeding and feeding areas is not known, humpbacks that winter in Hawaii generally travel to the coast of southeastern Alaska and south-central Alaska to feed. Those that winter off Mexico feed offshore from central California to Washington. Some of the whales that breed in Mexico travel to Alaska to feed as well.

The whales are studied by scientists on their feeding grounds, and observed by a growing number of whalewatchers, especially in Glacier Bay, Alaska. Humpbacks can be encountered singly or in spectacular, cooperative feeding groups as they gorge themselves on the abundant fish and zooplankton.

SOUTHERN MIGRATION: SEPTEMBER–FEBRUARY

The humpbacks' 3,000-mile (4,800 km) journey south begins as early as mid-September. If the North Pacific humpbacks follow a migration sequence similar to that of humpbacks in the southern hemisphere, females still nursing their nearly year-old calves are the first to initiate the move to the breeding grounds, followed by older juveniles, mature males, and non-pregnant females, with pregnant females bringing up the rear. No one knows for certain the details or the route of the North Pacific humpbacks. Experts are fairly certain that breeding—and possibly some births—occurs along the way. The optimum location for birth would be the more sheltered areas off the coasts of Mexico and Hawaii, where mothers and calves are better protected from storms and predators. Even after nearly 100 years of study, however, some of these particulars remain unknown. In contrast with the similarly observed gray whale, neither the mating nor the birth of a humpback has been recorded on film or described in the scientific literature.

Humpbacks arrive in the Hawaiian Islands, off the Big Island of Hawaii, as early as October. By late February, the flow of migrating humpbacks has increased to its maximum, with whales observable from all of the main islands. It is more difficult to see humpbacks from shore in other parts of the Pacific, but peak numbers of whales can be seen off western Mexico and the nearby islands of the Revillagigedos, Tres Marias, and Isabela.

By this time, the breeding grounds are transformed by whale activity. The acrobatic humpbacks engage in breaching, tail slapping, and pec-slapping. Males exhibit aggressive behavior toward one another, striving for position as the primary "escort" of a receptive female. Such a pod, usually comprising a single female and numerous males, will appear as a boil of activity. As the males pursue the female, one will displace the rest and maintain his position for several hours or longer; this activity is referred to as a "heat run." Humpback breeding strategy is polygamous: a male or female will mate with more than one partner of the opposite sex during a given breeding season.

CALVING SEASON:
DECEMBER–APRIL

Like many other migratory animals (and some humans), many whales head south for the winter. Females that have been impregnated the previous winter need a birthing place with warm waters and protection from winter storms. Hawaii and Mexico are the destinations for females ready to birth, courting whales, and an unknown number of immature whales. Both males and females reach sexual maturity after four to six years. Although females usually breed every two or even three years, quite often a female and a new calf are observed being chased at high speed by as many as 20 suitors, with much thrashing of water. A small number of mothers have been observed calving every year, but the survival rate of the calves is unknown. Synchronized perfectly with the annual migration, the gestation of the calf takes an average of 11½ months.

Humpback mothers are extremely nurturing of their new calves. A mother might caress or enfold her young with her pectoral fins, lie at the surface with the baby on her belly, or even buoy the baby clear of the water on top of her head! Before humpbacks were protected by law, whalers attracted a mother whale by attacking her baby—invariably, she would rush to the young one's aid. Humpbacks nurse their young slightly longer than most other baleen whales do (up to a year), although the youngster is feeding on solids during the latter months of lactation. The young are born with very thin blubber, so they must remain in the breeding grounds long enough to acquire adequate sustenance from the mother's rich milk (40–50 percent fat). By the time the mother-calf pair is ready to leave the breeding grounds, the baby has been transformed from a light gray, slightly wrinkled, sleek whale no bigger than one of its mother's pectoral fins to a robust, dark gray calf nearly half its mother's length.

RETURNING HOME:
MARCH–JULY

Even though a few stragglers arrive in the breeding grounds as late as February, the trip north seems to begin in early March. If the migratory segregation of northern humpbacks does mimic that of the southern Pacific whales, the newly pregnant females are likely to be in the lead, followed by juveniles, then mature males, with mother-calf pairs returning last. It is just as likely, however, that northern humpbacks migrate in mixed sex and age classes, with the young learning the migration from their mothers. In Hawaiian waters, during some years, it appears as if a wave of departure occurs toward the end of March, with large groups of whales heading north. Late in May and even into early summer, mother-calf pairs are observed just leaving the calving grounds, having given their young ample time to gain weight and strength for the sojourn back to the icy northern waters. Some whales find enough food to spend the summer in the Gulf of California, in the more nutrient-rich eastern North Pacific. Whales that head north may travel at an average speed of 2 knots, making the nearly 3,000-mile (4,800 km) trip in fewer than 80 days. Once in their feeding grounds, the humpbacks begin the annual cycle again, feeding and resting after their intensely active winter.

Hunting the Humpback Whale

What we have done to the great whales in the sacred name of commerce
is an affront to human dignity and a debasement of human values and
sensibility. These magnificent animals—almost certainly the largest
that have ever existed on earth, and now recognised as the possessors of
outstanding intelligence—have been brought to the brink of extinction
by killing methods of appalling cruelty.

—Sir Peter Scott (1909–1989)

Humpbacks were among the earliest whale species hunted
by humans. Because they feed and calve near the shore, hunting them did not require long, perilous trips out to sea. The
Japanese and many Northern and Eastern Pacific aboriginal
peoples engaged in shore-based whaling for centuries before
Europeans and New Englanders entered Pacific waters. The
Aleuts, Eskimos, and natives of Vancouver Island and the
Queen Charlotte Islands pursued whales, venturing forth in
wooden canoes or skin-covered kayaks.

It wasn't until the early nineteenth century that European
and Yankee whalers began plying the Pacific waters. By then,
two hundred years of whaling had taken their toll on the populations of Atlantic humpbacks and other species, forcing the
whalers to venture farther south and west in search of prey.
Initially, the whalers primarily pursued sperm and bowhead
whales, taking the North Pacific humpbacks only sporadically
off the west coast of North America, in bays along the west
coast of Mexico, in Japan, Korea, and the Marianas.

The pioneers who traveled overland to California found prac-
tically untouched stocks of humpbacks migrating along the
coastline. In 1851, a shore-based whaling station was estab-
lished at Monterey. Soon other stations opened, operating from
Half Moon Bay, California, to Point Abanda in Baja California.
Around the same time, in the mid-1850s, at least five American

25

companies were set up in Hawaii, specifically for the taking of humpbacks. (Prior to the 1850s, no record exists of humpback whales in the islands, so it is assumed that they are relative newcomers to Hawaiian shores.)

Because of diminishing whale stocks and a decline in the value of whale oil, whaling efforts in the Pacific were largely abandoned by the end of the nineteenth century. A shore-based whaling station did go into operation near Eureka, California, in 1939, but it closed soon after. Another station operated out of Richmond, California, from 1954 to 1973, taking approximately 800 humpbacks.

The advent of modern whaling technology in the twentieth century—exploding harpoons, steam and diesel-powered vessels, and factory ships—made profitability in the industry once again feasible. Far-reaching Antarctic whaling became a bonanza, and the humpback species faced extinction.

It was not until 1966 that the humpback was named an endangered species and given full protection from commercial fishing. By then, the estimated original world stocks of around 150,000 animals had been diminished to something less than today's estimations of between 10,000 and 15,000. During the heyday of the whaling era (nearly the entirety of the nineteenth century), an estimated 28,000 humpbacks were killed in the North Pacific alone. Today, subsistence whaling by native fisheries, which takes a few animals each year, is still permitted at Bequia in the Grenadines, in Greenland, and in the Cape Verde Islands.

Saving Humpbacks

Whaling, more than anything else, has been responsible for depleting the world population of humpbacks. But with protection from commercial hunting since 1966, humpbacks are showing some signs of recovery. It's estimated that several thousand now live in the North Pacific (where 12,000 to 15,000 once lived); some researchers believe the current population is even higher.

Each year, breeding/calving waters come alive with the presence of a new generation of baby humpbacks, visible in protected habitat in Hawaii, where the majority of the herd congregrate. Of course, it is highly important that calves are born, but it is equally important that they survive. At present, researchers are concerned about the survival of the calves, particularly since the whales migrate where hazardous fishing nets are extensively deployed.

The 1991 National Oceanic and Atmospheric Administration (NOAA) Recovery Plan for the Humpback Whale reported that humpbacks might never regain the population levels that prevailed before commercial hunting. The plan proposed doubling the population in 20 years (a difficult task), stating:

"For better or worse, humans have claimed an increasing share of the habitat and resources once available to humpbacks and other species. Humpback whales (living in the ocean for millions of years) have no alternative but to share the oceans with humans and exist in lower numbers. In contrast, it is only through force of law that humans must share the oceans with the humpback whales."

Humpbacks and many other marine animals face serious problems, including shortage of food as well as human-created problems such as noise, plastic waste, pollution, nets, and ocean mining. All of these factors threaten habitat with degradation or destruction. The whales' future and all life on earth depend on the health and safety of the planet's ecosystems. The challenge lies in developing a conscientious stewardship of these ecosystems, for, as much as we may love whales as individuals, as a society we are still killing them. Protection of habitat is the key; the hope for the whales lies in our realization that they need and deserve our protection.

Whalewatching from Shore

During certain parts of their migration cycle—especially during breeding season—humpbacks can be viewed from shore. During the rest of their migration cycle, shore-based viewing is almost impossible, as the whales are too far at sea. Below are some tips for whalewatching from shore.

1. Be aware of your environment. In the tropical breeding grounds of Hawaii, very little clothing is needed, but bottled sunscreen and some sort of shade or a hat will add greatly to your comfort. Weather off Mexico and Baja can be cooler and a light jacket may be necessary. The humpbacks' northern feeding grounds are considerably cooler, even in summer, and dressing in layers is always a good idea. Daytime temperatures can range from warm and comfortable to cold and rainy, so be prepared for all possibilities.

2. Bring binoculars or a high-powered spotter's scope (somewhat like a telescope, but of lesser power, available at some sporting goods stores). Although most photography is best from a boat, bring a camera in case whales come very close to shore. A telephoto lens is a must for serious photographers or for whale identification.

3. Look for blows just below the horizon. They stand out very well against other islands and when skies are overcast. Sometimes the whale's body will glint in the sunlight as it comes up for air or goes under for a dive. When a humpback breaches, a huge splash can be seen for many miles. Keep watching — they often breach more than once.

4. Mother-calf pairs seem to swim slightly closer to shore in the morning than later in the day. The sea is usually calmer in the morning hours, too. Blows and breaches become harder to see as wind stirs up whitecaps.

Whalewatching by Boat

Every year, boatloads of people pursue whales in hopes of shooting them—with their cameras. Watching whales from their own watery habitat is one of the best ways to view the whales and to foster stewardship of them.

In many parts of the humpbacks' range, whalewatching vessels are available for day trips during feeding and breeding seasons, with excellent long-term excursions available to Alaska and the Gulf of California. Many whalewatching vessels are based in Hawaii. Boats that offer the highest-caliber learning experience and operate with the most consideration for the whales usually carry a naturalist aboard. Because Hawaii is where federal whalewatching laws were first implemented, most experienced boat operators there have mastered the art of whalewatching at a protective distance from the whales.

Remember that the air is always cooler over water than over land; dress in layers. In the North Pacific, it can be quite cold onboard a vessel several miles at sea, and gloves, a hat, and a parka are often necessary, even in summer. Though usually pretty calm, weather off Maui can change completely within a few hours. A hat for sun protection is a good idea, with a light windbreaker for evening trips. Check with your excursion operator about proper equipment; some vessels rent binoculars. Many creatures besides whales live in or on the sea, so bring seabird, fish, and marine-mammal field guides if you have them. Plan to get wet if you go on a boat, be flexible, and expect to have the time of your life!

PRECAUTIONS FOR BOATERS

In order to assist the endangered humpback in its recovery, the governments of Canada, Mexico, and the United States have passed laws restricting activity both in breeding and in feeding ranges. Commonsense guidelines for most areas follow, in addition to the laws for Hawaiian waters.

1. Boats should approach humpbacks slowly, coming in from the side and slightly behind them, and slowing to match the speed of the slowest individual in a parallel course.

2. Vessels operated at a constant speed seem to disturb whales less than those that make frequent changes in speed or direction. Whales must be allowed to take the lead and should not be approached closer than 100 yards (91 m).

3. Boats should never be used to separate a mother and a calf, or to herd or drive whales. When approached carefully, with respect, whales may exhibit interest in the vessel and come closer to investigate. When they choose to approach a vessel, this is considered volitional on their part and not a boater's violation of the law.

4. If whales exhibit aggressive behavior or perform evasive maneuvers such as prolonged dives or course changes, the vessel should drop back or break off contact.

In Hawaii, federal regulations regarding humpback whales state that it is unlawful to:

1. Operate any aircraft within 1,000 feet (305 m) of a humpback whale;

2. Approach by any means closer than 100 yards (91 m) to any humpback whale, or within 300 yards (274 m) in cow/calf waters;

3. Cause a vessel or other object to approach within 100 yards (91 m) of a humpback whale, or within 300 yards (274 m) in cow/calf waters;

4. Disrupt or alter the normal behavior or activity of a humpback whale (for example, cause the whale to change direction rapidly or attempt to escape; interrupt breeding, nursing, or resting activities; etc.).

These laws apply to swimmers and windsurfers, as well as to any type of human-propelled craft, including kayaks.

Photographing Humpbacks

More and more, people are taking pictures of whales, instead of taking their lives, learning to appreciate these magnificent, endangered beings through firsthand experience. It takes a lucky shot, most often combined with skill and some fine equipment, to get a good photograph of a whale. However, here are a few tips that may improve your chances.

When aboard a boat, the main trick is to hold the camera as steady as possible. High film and fast shutter speeds will minimize blur in your still photos. When observing surface-active pods, remember that activities such as breaching may be performed repeatedly; you may get a second or third chance. Fluke displays are common among humpbacks; the fluke is probably the most photographed part of the whale. Watch for the moment when the whale prepares to dive. Its body often rises and rounds out into a hump at the surface—that's the moment to point the lens or roll the video. Right after that, humpbacks will often kick up their tails as they dive. Be prepared to shoot the huge flukes right at the surface of the water.

FLUKE IDENTIFICATION

By photographing flukes, researchers have identified over 1,000 individuals in the North Pacific herd. If you find you have taken a fluke shot, you can contribute to the valuable tracking of whale movements and the creation of life histories of individuals. Please send copies of your fluke shots to:

>Sally Mizroch
>National Marine Mammal Laboratory
>NOAA/NMFS/NWAFC
>7600 Sand Point Way NE, Bldg. 4
>Seattle, WA 98115

Include your name, the location of the humpbacks, date and time of photo, number of whales sighted (calves and adults), and what direction they were headed. Please note whether photos were taken from a boat (and the boat's name) or from shore. Include your telephone number and address if you wish.

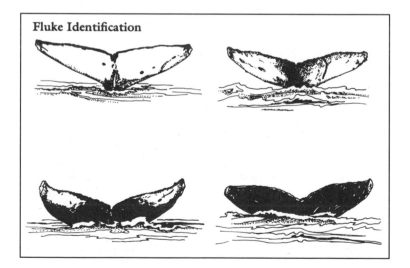

Fluke Identification

Whalewatching Guide

Following are listings of suggested whalewatching sites, arranged geographically, north to south and east to west, by state and province. Each listing is numbered for easy location on an accompanying map and includes a short description of the whalewatching site, information on best viewing, suggested resources, and other helpful hints.

Remember, whales are wild animals, and they may or may not show up during your watch. Patience is one of the essential elements in successfully watching whales in the wild. Humpback range covers some of the most spectacular scenery in the North Pacific; carrying appropriate field guides to the area you visit will enhance your experience and open your eyes to the incredible diversity of life all around you.

The following suggestions may help you locate a reliable tour-boat operator:

1. In small towns, contact the tourist information center or check around the harbor in person.

2. In larger cities, the Yellow Pages of the telephone book are a good resource. Try looking under Environmental Associations, Fishing Parties, Museums, Tour Operators, Charters, and Tourist Information. The local aquarium, zoo, or college may also provide references.

Final note: Should you know of additional good whalewatching sites not found in this book, please let Sasquatch Books know!

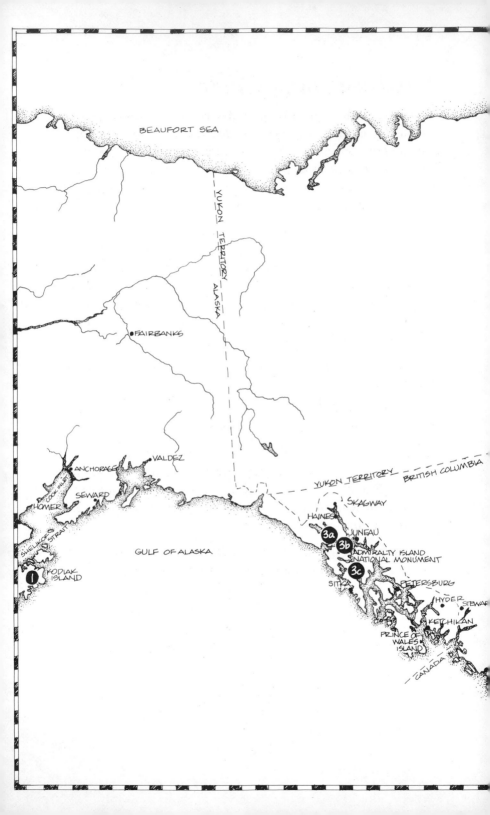

Alaska

Both southeastern and south-central Alaska are well-known feeding grounds for humpbacks. The whales were once so abundant in these areas that this was thought to be the major summering grounds in the North Pacific, and shore-based whaling stations took advantage of the whales' numbers. Although there are far fewer humpbacks to see in this region now, whalewatching by boat can be a fruitful venture. Before embarking on a journey to see feeding humpbacks in this area, check with the Alaska State Ferry System and the Alaska Division of Tourism in Juneau. There are many good cruise lines and outfitters to choose from.

1. KODIAK ISLAND. Humpbacks may be seen in the coastal waters of Kodiak Island. Their diagnostic features and feeding behavior easily distinguish them from gray whales, which also migrate through these waters. Kodiak City has accommodations for travelers, and a list of these can be obtained from the Kodiak Chamber of Commerce. To get to the island, take a ferry from Homer or Seward, or catch a flight from Anchorage.

2. PRINCE WILLIAM SOUND. In the summer months, humpbacks may be found near Naked and Chenega islands; in Perry Passage, Jackpot, Icy and Whale bays, and Port Bainbridge; and north of Montague Island.

3. INSIDE PASSAGE. Glacier Bay (3a), Icy Strait (3b), and Chatham Strait (3c) seem to be favorite areas for whales that are newly returned to the feeding grounds. At Glacier Bay, it is sometimes possible to see humpbacks from shore. The ferries that traverse these waters are good viewing platforms, as are the cruise ships that put into nearby ports-of-call.

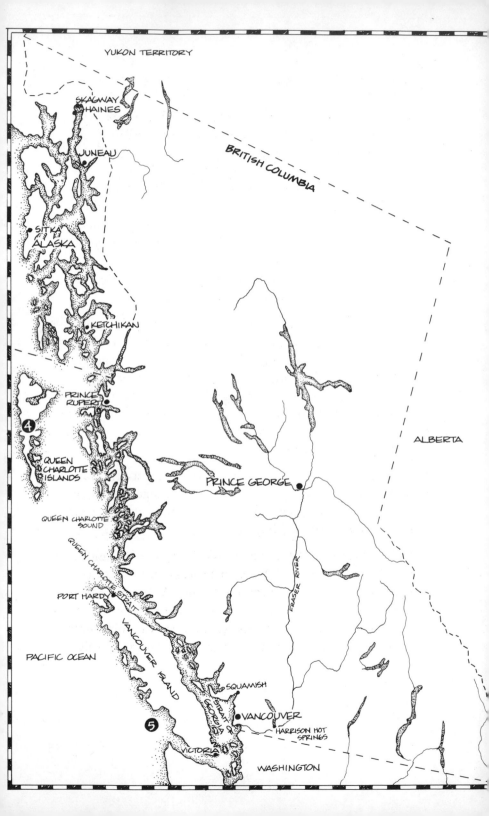

British Columbia

Although humpbacks were historically abundant along this scenic coast, today they are uncommon in comparison with points north and south, such as southeastern Alaska and northern California. Researchers have studied small numbers of whales in these waters, and humpbacks have been observed feeding here. Whalewatching from a vessel is a must.

4. QUEEN CHARLOTTE ISLANDS. The best whalewatching period here is from late spring through early summer. Gray and killer whales may be seen in this area at the same time. To obtain information about onboard whalewatching, contact the British Columbia Ministry of Tourism.

5. VANCOUVER ISLAND. Whalewatching charters are available on the east side at Victoria, and on the west side at Pacific Rim National Park. Catch a flight from Vancouver to Tofino Airport to get to the park, or a ferry from Port Alberni. For more details, write: Superintendent, Pacific Rim National Park, Box 280, Ucluelet, B.C., VOR 3AO.

Washington, Oregon, and California

The coasts of these states are summering grounds for humpbacks, and the whales move about quite a bit between the Gulf of the Farallones (off California) and Washington. In California humpbacks are found close to shore—within 100 fathoms of water.

6. WASHINGTON AND OREGON. Humpback whales are generally farther offshore in this region and not visible from land. No humpback whalewatching excursions operate out of Washington or Oregon.

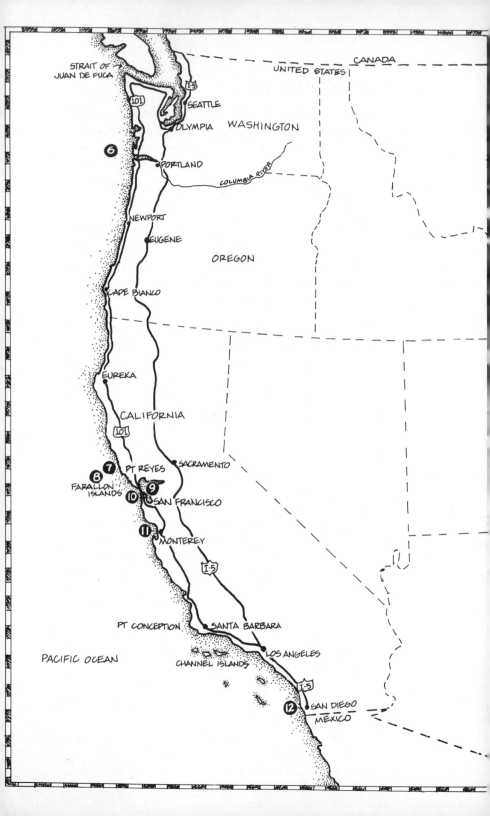

7. POINT REYES NATIONAL SEASHORE. Take Sir Francis Drake Boulevard from Highway 101 to the end, or take Highway 1 to Olema and follow the signs. A short walk to the stairway leading up to the lighthouse provides a rewarding view.

8. FARALLON ISLANDS. This National Wildlife Refuge is not open to the public, but whales that feed in this area may be observed from boats out of San Francisco. Oceanic Society Expeditions runs nature trips to the Farallon Islands through the summer and fall seasons. More information on the islands can be obtained from the U.S. Fish and Wildlife Service, P.O. Box 524, Newark, CA 94560.

9. SAN FRANCISCO BAY. Although humpbacks rarely enter the bay, in 1985 a famous whale made several forays in, with one spectacular trip nearly 20 miles (32 km) up the Sacramento River Delta. "Humphrey the Humpback" was finally coaxed out to sea by the recorded sounds of feeding humpbacks. Humphrey has been sighted many times in the Gulf of the Farallones since his rescue.

10. HALF MOON BAY. Whalewatching trips are conducted from this harbor during the gray whale migration. There is a slight chance of seeing migrating humpbacks as well. Contact Oceanic Society Expeditions for more information.

11. MONTEREY BAY. Although humpbacks don't travel close to shore in this area (unlike grays), several excellent boat excursions conduct nature trips during which you may see whales. Oceanic Society Expeditions conducts week-long humpback whale and dolphin research expeditions in the summer and fall.

12. SAN DIEGO. Several kinds of expeditions leave from San Diego for the Mexican breeding grounds. Contact the American Cetacean Society for more information.

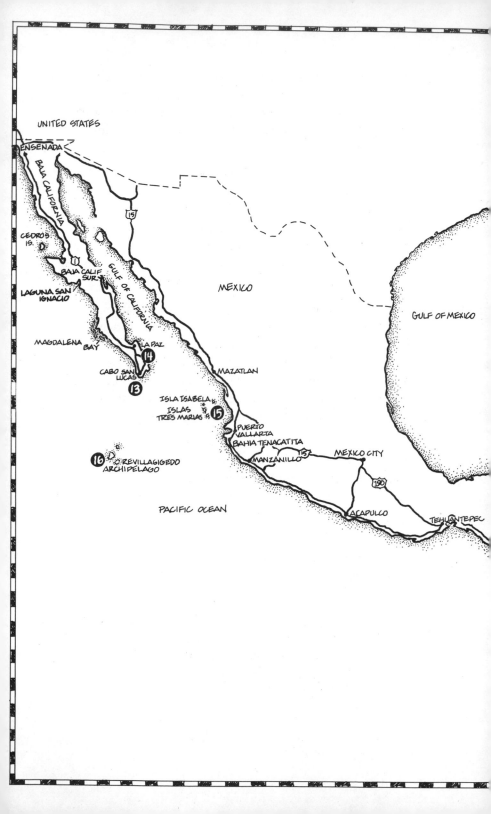

Mexico

Unless you have a tremendous amount of experience or a lot of luck, you are far less likely to see humpbacks from shore than from a boat. The Mexican government has designated many of the western lagoons of Baja as gray whale calving sanctuaries. Humpbacks do not tend to enter these lagoons, but they abound farther offshore along much of the Mexican coast. Several excellent outfitters conduct week-long trips, departing from the following Mexican ports.

13. CABO SAN LUCAS. At the tip of Baja, "Cabo" has become a popular destination for individuals seeking a tropical respite. Many charter dive-boats double as whale-watching vessels during the winter.

14. LA PAZ. The harbor at La Paz on the east coast of Baja is the site of departure for several long-term whalewatching expeditions. Arrangements can be made for trips departing from La Paz through the Baja Expeditions office located there.

15. MEXICAN MAINLAND (Mazatlan to Tehuantepec, including Isla Isabela, Islas Tres Marias, and Bahia de Banderas at Puerto Vallarta). Obviously, a boat is needed to see the whales that congregate around the islands, but whales are occasionally sighted from land at Bahia Tenacatita, Manzanillo, and Puerto Vallarta.

16. REVILLAGIGEDO ARCHIPELAGO (including Islas Socorro, San Benedicto, and Clarion). Some week-long expeditions run out to these islands from La Paz, but most of them are fishing trips. Inquire with Oceanic Society Expeditions for more information.

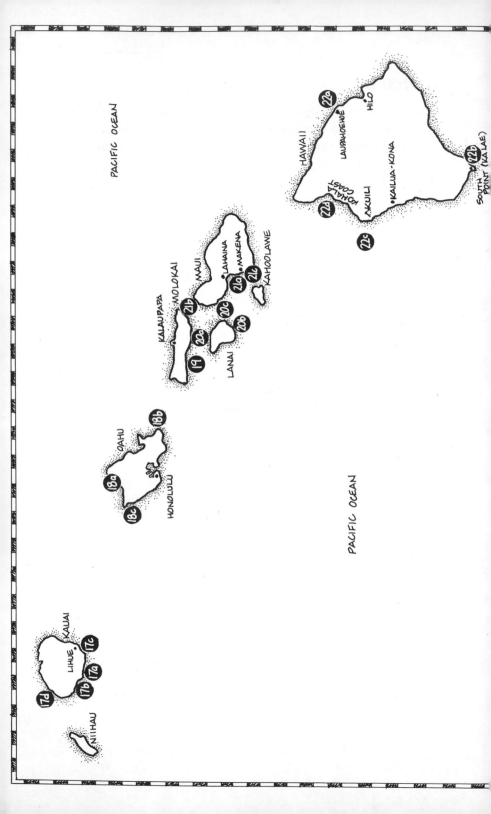

Hawaii

Each winter, hundreds of humpbacks pass through the Hawaiian archipelago. Your chances of seeing the whales from land or sea are better here than anywhere else in the North Pacific. Because the islands are volcanic and rise relatively steeply from the water, it is often easy to find an elevated spot from which to look for whales. It doesn't take much elevation to see several miles or more out to sea, yet the whales will come within several hundred yards of shore in some places. There are also many day trips offered on commercial charter boats. Oceanic Society Expeditions conducts week-long expeditions to humpback breeding grounds.

17. KAUAI. Several tour boats operate out of Hanalei, but whales can be seen fairly easily from land. They come within 500 yards (457 m) of shore between Port Allen (17a) and Kekaha (17b), and are visible from the road (please pull off in a safe area before looking). Additional viewing sites are found along the south shore between Makahuena Point (17c) and Kekaha, and at Polihale State Park (17d) on the west side.

18. OAHU. The frequency of whale sightings has gradually increased all around this island. Some locations that have proved fruitful for viewing are Pupakea (18a), Makapuu (18b), and Kaena Point (18c). Several excursion vessels leave Honolulu Harbor daily.

19. MOLOKAI. For whale observation, the harbor of Kaunakakai on one side and the peninsula of Kalaupapa on the other bracket the island. Land owned by Molokai Ranch may be accessible by advance arrangement; contact the Activities Manager, Jay Anderson, P.O. Box 8, Maunaloa, HI 96770 (808-552-2767).

20. LANAI. Best viewing points are along the eastern shore, from Shipwreck Beach (20a) to Manele Bay (20b), with Lanai Landing and Keomuku (20c) in between. It is a short hop from Maui to Lanai, and ferry service operates from Lahaina throughout the day. Many commercial excursion vessels also visit Lanai.

21. MAUI. Undoubtedly the capital of whalewatching in the Hawaiian Islands and perhaps the whole North Pacific. The protected waters between the neighboring islands of Molokai, Lanai, and Kahoolawe are particularly rich with whales each winter. Many day trips run out of Lahaina and Maalaea harbors (21a) on the west side. Some of the larger operators offer naturalist-narrated trips and even contribute a portion of their profits to whale conservation. If you go on a smaller vessel, be wary of anyone promising to get you "right up on the whales"—that is harassment and it is illegal. On Maui, almost anyplace you can see the water, you are likely to see whales. Especially good viewing occurs from Kapalua (21b) south to Maalaea Bay all the way to Makena (21c) on the west and south sides. There are many pull-outs and viewpoints along the way, so be a conscientious driver and pull over before you look!

22. HAWAII. In general, roads are set farther back on the "Big Island," or they lie at sea level without good sightlines to the water. Pull-out access is more limited as well. Nonetheless, whales can sometimes be seen from some places on land. On the east side, Laupahoehoe Lookout (22a) is a good vantage point, as is the Hilo Breakwater. South Point (22b) comes closer to the water. On the west side, the Kuili cinder cone offers a commanding view (22c). Whales can be sighted from high points and shore lookouts along the Kohala Coast (22d), particularly at Spencer Beach Park. Boat excursions are the best bet for seeing humpbacks, and several operate out of Kailua-Kona.

WHALE SIGHTING LOG

LOCATION	DATE & TIME	WEATHER	SEA CONDITION	# OF WHALES IN GROUP	DIRECTION OF TRAVEL

NOTES:

_____

_____

_____

_____

_____

_____

_____

_____

_____

Suggested Readings

Ken Balcomb III, *The Whales of Hawaii* (San Francisco: Marine Mammal Fund, 1987).

Robert Burton, *The Life and Death of Whales* (Totowa, N.J.: Rowman & Allanheld, 1980).

Tim Dietz, *Whales and Man: Adventures with the Giants of the Deep* (Dublin, N.H.: Yankee Publishing, Inc., 1987).

C. D'Vincent, D. Haley, and F. Sharpe, *Voyaging with the Whales* (Toronto: Boulton Publishing Services, 1989).

Francois Gohier, *Humpback Whales: Traveling on the Wings of Sound* (San Luis Obispo: Blake Publishing, 1991).

Gregory D. Kaufman and Paul H. Forestell, *Hawaii's Humpback Whales: A Complete Whalewatchers Guide* (Kihei, Hawaii: Pacific Whale Foundation Press, 1986).

S. Leatherwood, R. R. Reeves, and L. Foster, *The Sierra Club Handbook of Whales and Dolphins* (San Francisco: Sierra Club Books, 1983).

S. Leatherwood, R. R. Reeves, W. F. Perrin, and W. E. Evans, *Whales, Dolphins, and Porpoises of the Eastern North Pacific and Adjacent Arctic Waters: A Guide to Their Identification* (Mineola, N.Y.: Dover Publications, Inc., 1988).

Anthony Martin, *The Illustrated Encyclopedia of Whales and Dolphins* (New York: Portland House, 1990).

Joan McIntyre, *The Delicate Art of Whale Watching* (New York: Random House, 1991).

Tsuneo Nakamura, *Gentle Giant: At Sea with the Humpback Whale* (San Francisco: Chronicle Books, 1984).

F. Nicklin, K. Norris, and J. Darling, *With the Whales* (Minocqua, Wis.: NorthWord Press, Inc., 1990).

Spencer W. Tinker, *Whales of the World* (Honolulu: Bess Press, Inc., 1988).

Lois K. Winn and Howard E. Winn, *Wings in the Sea: the Humpback Whale* (Hanover: University Press of New England, 1985).

BOOKS FOR CHILDREN

Ernest Callenbach, *Humphrey the Wayward Whale* (Berkeley: Heyday Books, 1986).

Gill McBarnet, *The Whale Who Wanted to Be Small* (Puunene, Hawaii: Ruwanga Trading, 1985).

———, *A Whale's Tale* (Puunene, Hawaii: Ruwanga Trading, 1988).

———, *The Wonderful Journey* (Puunene, Hawaii: Ruwanga Trading, 1986).

Bruce McMillan, *Going on a Whale Watch* (New York: Scholastic, Inc., 1992).

Robert Siegel, *Whalesong* (San Francisco: HarperCollins, 1981).

———, *White Whale* (San Francisco: HarperCollins, 1991).

Information Sources

ALASKA

Alaska State Museum
395 Whittier Street
Juneau, AK 99801

University of Alaska
  Museum
907 Yukon Drive
Fairbanks, AK 99701

BRITISH COLUMBIA

Vancouver Public Aquarium
P.O. Box 3232
Vancouver, B.C. V6B 3X8

West Coast Whale Foundation
1040 W. Georgia Street
Suite 2020
Vancouver, B.C. V6E 4H1

CALIFORNIA

The American
Cetacean Society
P.O. Box 2639
San Pedro, CA 90731

California Academy of
Sciences/Steinhart Aquarium
Golden Gate Park
San Francisco, CA 94118

California Marine
Mammal Center
Fort Cronkhite
Sausalito, CA 94965

Monterey Bay Aquarium
886 Cannery Row
Monterey, CA 93940

Oceanic Society Expeditions
Fort Mason Center, Bldg. E
San Francisco, CA 94123

HAWAII

Center for Whale Studies
39 Woodvine Court
Covington, LA 70433
during winter months:
P.O. Box 1539
Lahaina, HI 96767

Earthtrust
Save the Whales International
25 Kaneohe Bay Drive
Kailua, HI 96734

University of Hawaii
1000 Pope Road
Honolulu, HI 96822

MEXICO

Departmento de Biologica
Facultad de Ciencias
Universidad Nacional
Autonoma de Mexico
Apdo. Postal 70-572
04510 Mexico, D.F., Mexico

OREGON

Marine Science Center
Oregon State University
2030 S. Marine Science Drive
Newport, OR 97365

WASHINGTON

Cascadia Research Collective
Water Street Bldg., Suite 201
218½ W. Fourth Avenue
Olympia, WA 98501

Center for Whale Research
P.O. Box 1577
Friday Harbor, WA 98250

The Whale Museum
P.O. Box 945
Friday Harbor, WA 98250